I AM
Praying For You

Written by
Janet Oyebode

I AM Praying for You

Copyright © 2020 by JanetOyebode

All rights reserved. No portion of this book may be reproduced, used, or transmitted in any form or by any means, electronic or mechanical, including photocopying, recording, or by any information storage or retrieval system, without express written permission, with the exception of brief excerpts in articles or reviews, etc. The scanning, uploading, and distribution of this book without permission is a theft of the author's intellectual property. If you would like permission to use material from the book (other than for review purposes), please contact jejerinle792@gmail.com. Thank you for your support of the author's rights.

ISBN: 0-9701591-3-7

Scripture quotations marked (KJV) are takenfrom the *Holy Bible*, King James Version.

The information given in this book is given withthe understanding the author is not engaged in rendering legal, professional advice.

Book coordination by Get The Pen
Email: janine.folks@gmail.com

Cover design by: www.dhartdesign.net
Email: art_design@dhartdesign.net.

I AM Praying for You

Dedication

This book is dedicated to the memory of my beloved elder brother, Adeoye Erinle.

~ I was once told, all healing may not occur on this side of eternity, but certainly complete healing on the other side. GOD knows it was His plan, sickness free indeed!!!

I AM Praying for You

Foreword

By the grace of God, pastor Janet Oyebode has written for us a gem value to those whose hearts are alive to God, and who look to Him for help. Her background in the church and charity ministries recommends her highly, and no doubt has enabled her to produce this short but weighty work. The section where she prays for readers is a precious gift because "the effectual (focused) fervent prayer of the righteous avails much" - James 5:16. The Confessions remind God's children of the necessity of confessing not only their faith, but also, always, the Word of God, in order to bring into existence, all those things promised by their Father. "With the heart man believes and with the mouth confession is made unto salvation (in all its ramifications) - Romans 10:10. This is extremely important because of the supremacy that God has put upon His word. "You have exalted Your Word above all Your Name" - Psalm 138:2. The author's salutations and passionate entreaties to the Holy Spirit show the kind of intimate relationship that all children of God are expected to have with this third Person of the God-head. He is the executor of all the purposes of God, and our enabler in all godly things. Notwithstanding the emphasis on the Word of God, He gave us His Names (or multifaceted

I AM Praying for You

Name), to work with. There are multiple covenant Names of God, and the author distils a number of them into powerful, situation-changing prayers for the benefit of the reader.

Finally, the author braces up the readers with Words of Encouragement. Many observers have pointed out that in today's world with its abundance of adversities, what most people need is encouragement. This need is succinctly and strongly met in this section.

Without a doubt, this book will quickly take its rightful place in the collection of extremely useful faith-building and faith-sustaining resources which are available to the Christians and seekers alike. I highly recommend it to all.

Emmanuel Ayorinde, Ph.D, PE.
Wayne State University, Detroit, Michigan, USA

Acknowledgement

This book would not have been possible without the love and support of family and friends.

I wish to express my deepest gratitude to Dr. Emmanuel Ayorinde, my spiritual father, who read the manuscript, offered suggestions, and wrote the forward to this book. What a gift you are to me and the Body of Christ! Thank you sir.

My profound gratitude to Janine Folks who made the process of writing and publishing this book a wonderful experience and a reality.

Special thanks to my husband who over the years has given me the confidence and space needed to grow and spread my wings in my work and passion of serving others in ministry.

To my children BJ and Krystal, my world would be void without you in it. Love you endlessly xx

I AM Praying for You

"True prayer is measured by weight, not by length. A single groan before God may have more fullness of prayer in it than a fine oration of great length."

-C.H. Spurgeon

"Prayer is bringing words from your heart to the throne of grace. It is more of the heart than the mouth. Engage your heart in prayer. If you don't engage your heart consciously, the heart will engage itself foolishly."

- Janet Oyebode

I AM Praying for You

Table of Contents

Dedication	3
Foreword by Emmanuel Ayorinde, Ph.D, PE. Wayne State University	4
Acknowledgement	6
About The Author - Janet Oyebode	9
Introduction	11
I. Prayers	13
II. Confession of the Day	34
III. Good Morning Holy Spirit	40
IV. Praying God's Name	45
V. Words of Encouragement	48
Testimonial	70

I AM Praying for You

About The Author

Janet Oyebode

Janet Oyebode became an ordained pastor in 2008 and serves alongside her husband, Snr Pastor and General Overseer James Oyebode at Just For Christ Ministries.

Pastor Janet relocated to the U.S from London, England in 1996. She and her husband are blessed with two adult children.

In addition to her church commitments, she is also the Founder and Executive Director of Hope Alive Outreach Center, a non-profit organization formed in May, 2015 and functions on the guidelines of Matthew 25:42-45. Through this organization she serves the homeless, the locked in and the shut out. With her recent partnership with Brilliant Detroit she now works to create kid success families where families with children 0-8 have what they need to be school ready, healthy and stable in high-need neighborhoods.

She is also the co-founder and president of Alliance of Women in Ministry. AWM is a Christian national and professional development organization of women that impact the Kingdom through teaching, supporting, encouraging and networking. They hope to empower, promote, inspire and develop women for the work of Jesus Christ.

Pastor Janet believes fiercely that, "We rise by lifting others and that together, we can make a difference!"

I AM Praying for You

Introduction

I have found that many today need words of encouragement to start their day and knowing that someone is praying for them has been a great source of comfort.

I joined Facebook 10 years ago as a ministry platform to share the Gospel of Christ and connect with other Christ followers. I soon found myself posting daily prayers and words of encouragement. Many told me how my daily posts were a blessing to them. There would be times I felt the need to take a break from Facebook and I could be off the platform for weeks. I would receive private messages asking me to come back because they were missing my daily posts. The first time that happened I was truly touched by how God was using me to reach His people by sharing words and prayers of hope.

This book is mostly a compilation of all my daily Facebook posts and words of encouragement through the years.

It's my hope that this book of prayer helps the reader to form a close and intimate relationship with Jesus. To develop a quiet time of focus that pays attention to God throughout the day. The demands of our daily grind and the struggles we experience often take our focus away from the Living God, who holds our destiny in His hands and is best to direct our path.

David understood the importance of quiet time with God. He had a set time when He would pray seven times a day (Psalm 119:164). It provided a way to keep his mind, heart and soul focused on the word and will of God. When we start our day with prayer we are able to command our morning and set the tone of how the day is going to be for us.

This book has chapters dedicated to Prayers, Confession of The Day, Good Morning Holy Spirit, Praying God's Name and Words of Encouragement.

I AM Praying for You

Prayers

As you read this book, may Testimonies surround you!!!

Heavenly Father, We know that there is no defeat in You, therefore we cannot be overtaken, nor shall we be moved. Today, I pray for all of my friends and family who may need a miracle. Some are facing difficulties that seem too hard to overcome, and things look hopeless. Give strength to those who are carrying a heavy burden today, replace their anxious thoughts with Your truth. Soothe their restless hearts with Your peace and give them comfort with Your presence. Let them know that in You alone our hope is found, and in Your master plan You are working everything for their good. In Jesus' mighty name!

Every failure at the verge of success, walking encircle and hard labour with no result, ends in your life today in Jesus' name.

Remember this - They can't fight GRACE and win! May everything go well with you this Week, in Jesus' Mighty Name!!!

Lord, let my life INSPIRE others!

I AM Praying for You

All of you and none of me …

No more lack, no more shame, no more limitations!!!

Everything written by God concerning you, is established. They'll manifest this Week in Jesus' Mighty Name.

I command every go slow and stagnation in your life to disappear in the name of Jesus!

May God make you a Kingdom Treasurer, and a magnet of Kingdom prosperity in Jesus' name.

You've waited on the LORD...
The World will soon announce your ARRIVAL, in Jesus' Name.

ONE little "Divine appointment" can change a life for eternity!

The Lord is my strength and my song; he has given me victory. (Psalms 118:14)

May you not be dethroned from your God given seat, in Jesus' name.

Create in me a clean heart, O God; and renew a right spirit within me. (Psalm 51:10)

I AM Praying for You

Thank You Lord for blocking everything that was created to destroy me...

Be encouraged by this truth:
"You have enclosed me behind and before, and laid Your hand upon me" (Psalm 139:5)

God has your front, back and sides. He has you covered. He makes a way where there is no way. You can trust Him!

Before I call, You will answer; and while I am yet speaking, You will hear. (Isaiah 65:24)

Because God is on your side, you'll Succeed in many ways. It's your Week, Prosper in Jesus Name!

I claim every goodness, favor, miracles and breakthrough that is attached to today in the name of Jesus.

May the Divine YES of God Almighty rest upon every desire of your heart in the name of Jesus.

The name of Jesus shall not fail over your case in the name of Jesus.

God Almighty will answer all powers asking "Where is your God?"

I AM Praying for You

Every trick and pain of the devil at the edge of your miracle shall not prosper, in the name of Jesus.

Lord, let the fruits of prayer grow and manifest in me in the name of Jesus.

Every arrow of shame and disgrace targeted at you, I fire back to sender in the name of Jesus.

Every demonic wall of partition between you and your breakthrough, be dashed to pieces in Jesus' name.

Lord, let the crown of marital success be placed on my head in the name of Jesus.

Angel of the living God, go and minister favor on my behalf in the hearts of my destiny helpers in the name of Jesus.

May you stand out amongst your peers. May all who see you confess with their mouth that God has indeed Blessed you ... In Jesus' Name.

If you love someone, pray for them. Pray for their peace. Pray for their growth. Pray for their success. Pray for their happiness.
I pray that you have all this and more.

I declare that the devourer will not hurt you, in Jesus' name.

GOD is going to get you out of a situation you once thought impossible.

When evil is present, know that GOOD is making a way for you.

You are the one who gives us victory over our enemies ; You disgrace those who hate Us! (Psalm 44:7)

Don't let your night discourage and destroy you. Weeping may endure for the night but JOY comes in the morning. Your end shall be Victorious... ENDURE!

Praise ye the LORD. Blessed is the man that feareth the LORD, that delighteth greatly in his commandments. His seed shall be mighty upon earth: the generation of the upright shall be blessed. (Psalms 112:1-2)

The Lord shall separate you from every power delaying the fulfillment of God's purposes in your life.

I AM Praying for You

Every ancient voice speaking against you:
In the name of Jesus, I silence and demolish that voice NOW!

Watch ye therefore, and pray always... (Luke 21:36)

This is my PRAYER AND HEARTCRY for every person on the face of this earth........ That we be found in the arms of Jesus when we breathe our last!!!

Your Blessings are Unstoppable!

You will not miss your miracle this year

Any foothold the enemy has in your life, O Lord, terminate them all.

Every storm is a school. Every trial is a teacher. Every experience is an education. Every difficulty is for your development. Romans 5:3-4 "We can rejoice when we run into problems and trials for we know that they are good for us - they help us learn to be patient. And patience develops strength of character in us and helps us trust God more each time."

May God hear the voice of His people, and save THEIR Land!

Remember to pray for our Nation!

I AM Praying for You

You will not be at the mercy of your mockers in the name of Jesus.

Command my miracle to overrule my mistakes. Let my miracle be a testimony to my family, friends and acquaintances worldwide.

STOP doubting God he heard you the first time! Praise him in advance it's done!

May God assist you to overcome every Red Sea, every valley... may you emerge favored and victorious because He has graced you with the fortitude NEVER to quit, in Jesus name.

I command every prison that is caging your PEACE to collapse by fire.
Arise and Shine in Jesus Name!

Make this your declaration from Matthew 16:19: Though the fig tree may not blossom, Nor fruit be on the vines; Though the labor of the olive may fail, And the fields yield no food; Though the flock may be cut off from the fold, And there be no herd in the stalls — Yet I will rejoice in the LORD, I will joy in the God of my salvation. (Habakkuk 3:17-18) ... Your worship filled resilience results in Divine Restitution! No matter what you're facing today, get up and say BLESSED BE THE NAME OF THE LORD!

I AM Praying for You

So then it is not of him who wills, nor of him who runs, but of God who shows mercy. (Romans 9:16).

May God unleash a fresh outpouring of His grace and goodness over your life. May He open Heaven's doors and pour out His Spirit in increasing measures. May He firmly establish you in His highest and best purposes for you. May you acquire such a taste for the presence of God that you're no longer tempted or distracted by cheap counterfeits and temporary sources. He is the One True God and He delights in every detail of your life. Have a blessed-power-FULL Day.

My God shall supply all your needs according to His riches in glory in Christ Jesus. (Philippians 4:19)

God's riches are endless and He really means it when He says, "I will supply ALL your needs." If we take this promise to heart, we need not fear or worry.

You are a city set on a hill. You will never be low again, in Jesus' name.

May all satanic manipulations through friends and family be dissolved, in Jesus' name.

Whatever makes you depressed and sad, I cast it out now in the name of Jesus.

I AM Praying for You

Heaven will smile on you this week...

Good news awaits you this month. You will be hearing "CONGRATULATIONS" from now, in Jesus' name!

Thank You Lord for the promise that You will meet our needs. Help us not to fear or doubt.

SUDDENLY...The World will see you at the TOP!!! SUDDENLY, God will do it for you!

That HELP you prayed for, is coming your way today!

May the OIL of Progress rest upon your household, in Jesus' name.

Every family that has been torn apart by the enemy: I declare from TODAY restoration and reconciliation, in the name of Jesus.

That problem you're facing right now can never defeat you because you're going to rise in the VICTORY of our Lord Jesus Christ.

That HELP you prayed for, is coming your way today.

I AM Praying for You

This is for someone: You are a danger zone to the devil

May the Lord make your life comfortable..

Every conspiracy concerning you is aborted, receive it by Grace.

Whoever digs a pit will fall into it, And he who rolls a stone will have it roll back on him. (Proverbs 26:27)

My prayer for you today: You will laugh in the face of the enemy!!!

Every Judas Iscariot in your life betraying and exposing your secrets to your enemies and friends alike, shall be exposed and disgraced in Jesus' name.

Every satanic embargo on your handwork be nullified in the name of Jesus.

If your goals are good, you will be respected, but if you are looking for trouble, that is what you will get. (Proverbs 11:27)

He restores my soul. (Psalm 23:3)

I AM Praying for You

Are you hurting today? Let God's love restore you. He always makes things better than they were before. Isaiah 25:8 "and the Lord God will wipe away tears from off all faces; "

"The Lord gave victory to David wherever He went." Receive "victory" today to go through any tests, trials, and circumstances you are in.

May God be your ever-present help in time of need.

Whatever makes you depressed and sad, I cast it out NOW in the name of Jesus.

Instead of going down, you are changing levels TODAY in Jesus name. You are going up!

Every sad and wicked diagnosis of disease, we reject it today in Jesus' name.

No more limitations or stagnation in the name of Jesus!

Every Spirit of delay I curse today, in the name of Jesus.

Whatever your heart desires, you shall not be barren of it. It is your season of Fruitfulness.

I command that opposition against you to bow, in the name of Jesus!

Today, you shall possess the gates of your enemies, in Jesus' name.

My prayer for you today: May you never find yourself in a situation where you have to borrow money. Henceforth, YOU shall be a lender/giver and not a borrower, in Jesus name.

The remaining Days of this Year...
I Pray the FULL RESTORATION of All Things the enemy has stolen from you, in Jesus' Mighty Name!

I release the angels to war on my behalf and dissipate any delay caused by the enemy. My God is for me and not against me.

I decree in Jesus' name that I will taste and see the goodness of the Lord in the land of the living!

You will LIVE and not die. You will make it in Jesus' name...

When my father and my mother forsake me, Then the Lord will take care of me. (Psalm 27:10)

I AM Praying for You

"For as he thinks in his heart, so is he." (Proverbs 23:7) ... Your thoughts are a precursor to your lifestyle.

May the blessings of Abraham locate you without delay, in Jesus' name.

As bad as it is, BE ENCOURAGED right now; satan wishes it was worse but God has limited what he can do. Thank God for His SPIRITUAL HEDGE of protection...

May every relationship God has ordained for you remain secured and every one sent by the enemy be permanently removed In Jesus' name.

The Lord has heard my supplication, the Lord accepts my prayer.

My prayer for you today: Every stronghold of failure be broken, in Jesus' name.

Receive explosive breakthroughs, I reject weak breakthroughs, in the name of Jesus.

Every unprofitable love targeted against me, be broken now, in the name of Jesus.

Without faith in God it is impossible to please God...

I AM Praying for You

Lifting up all those looking for the fruit of the womb... Like Hannah, God will hear your groaning and cries. He will remember you and take away your reproach... I prophesy, by this time next year the cries of babies shall be heard in your home.

No one will be a Crown-wearer in Heaven who isn't a Cross-bearer on Earth...

The eyes beholding this post .... God's about to SUPERsize your blessing, if you believe receive it in the name of Jesus.

There's a place waiting for you at the top, you will get there in Jesus' Name.

I plead the Blood stained banner of the LORD JESUS CHRIST over you right now .... touch, heal, set completely free in mind, heart, body, soul and spirit. According to: ISAIAH 53:4-5

Before the end of this month .... God will send you a NEW song, a SONG OF VICTORY in the name of Jesus.
The God of Justice will take on your case and Heaven will fight your fight, in Jesus' Name.

You can NEVER go wrong serving God!
Lord, let every unseen power that is troubling our

lives, no matter how close they are to us, BE DESTROYED COMPLETELY IN JESUS' NAME - AMEN!

May the Word of God become your dancing shoes and the music to your ears for the remainder of this year and beyond. That shall be your story in Jesus' name.

From today... Every song of sorrow you've been singing comes to an end. You shall sing a new song in the name of Jesus.

In every endeavor of life there are oppositions, hindrances; obstacles and obstruction...
Anyone who has put themselves in opposition against you shall fail shamefully, in the name of Jesus!

May The Angel of The Lord encamp around you for defense and protection, for support and up-liftment; for favor and blessing in the name of Jesus.

9 PM - 12 AM Second Prayer Watch: This is a special time in which divine favor from God and man is granted. When you talk to God, miracles happen. For someone tonight, it's a change of status. Receive your Divine Turnaround now in Christ Jesus name...

I AM Praying for You

There are dead things that are coming to life around you this week. There are dead parts of your body coming back to life, businesses and jobs coming back to life; promotions coming back to life, expectations coming back to life, in the Name of JESUS!

There's pressure on you and Sometimes you feel like everyone is against you and nobody cares. I'm here to remind you, God is a Promise Keeper.

May the hand of God never leave you in Jesus' name.

I rebuke the struggle, the shame; the disgrace, the embarrassment and I command the boldness of righteousness to be your new garment. Occupy your place in Christ in Jesus mighty name.

The enemy shall recall all assignments against your life and well being when he sees THE BLOOD, they will not stand but you shall stand in Jesus Mighty Name.

My prayer for you today... May God add color to your life, terminate every insult and turn your mistakes to miracles in Jesus' name.
There are some people who are friends with you for one reason To fight against you so they can use your past against your present From today, at this very hour let the heat of the Holy Ghost visit them

wherever they may be and expose them in Jesus' name.

Opening the Bible is not enough to conquer your enemies. You have to put the Word on your tongue. Your mouth is the gun and the Word your bullet.

Having the Shield of Faith is to fight and defend yourself through the Sword of The Spirit. To conquer and overcome you must have the Word of God in your mouth. KNOW AND SPEAK THE WORD... Selah!

Anything that is planning to cause you harm, from today God will expose it. When the devil plans his schemes in the corridor, God will reveal it to you in your bedroom.

Where others are struggling you will enter and excel. That which makes others common will make you STAND OUT. Where others fall short you will STAND TALL in Jesus' name.

CELEBRATION will overtake your entire destiny. Your dance will be unusual, you will shout a new shout and sing a new song because of the manifestation of the fullness of God in your life. It is done in Jesus' precious name.

I AM Praying for You

My prayer for you today... The expectations of your enemy is disappointed. EVERY conspiracy of darkness, EVERY satanic agenda and EVERY setup of wickedness is rendered null and void.

Even when your problems seem too much and unending ... I declare by the Power of The Holy Ghost, your inner Joy shall be bigger in Jesus' Mighty Name.

I speak to every storm in your life right now.... CEASE in the name of Jesus!!! Peace be still....... In your family Peace be still ..... In your finances Peace be still... In your marriage Peace be still..... EVERY STORM CEASE IN THE NAME OF JESUS!

Nobody but God brought me out so I owe no one but Him!!

"The Lord has done what he purposed; he has carried out his word, which he commanded long ago" (Lamentation 2:17)

I bind every evil spirit of mental illness. By Fire, by Force......... Demons are being cast out. Father release Your Spirit of soundness of mind to those afflicted now, in Jesus' name.

I AM Praying for You

The LOVE of God has taken you from a place of temporary to PERMANENT VICTORY over your adversaries, in Jesus' name.

Sometimes God will do it FOR you, other times He will do it THROUGH you. You are blessed to be a blessing to others.

When pain, sorrow, and despair cause the light of hope to flicker and burn low, communication with our Heavenly Father provides peace.

We hide behind a fake smile to mask the pain but sometimes we wish someone would look closely enough and see how broken we really are inside.

Luke 4:16-19 | | What is written is more important than what is happening because what is written has the power to overturn, overtake and overrule what is happening. Open The Book (Bible) and find the place where it has been written concerning you.
Embrace the power of the Written Word and be lifted to your next level.

As we look into the mirror to examine our hair and clothes... Let us look into the Scriptures to examine our soul! ~Hebrews 4:12

Jesus raised the dead... Healed the sick...
Turned water into wine... And walked on water!
Yes, I'm sure He can take care of you!!!

"My grace is sufficient for you, for my power is made perfect in weakness." ~2Cor. 12:9
Jesus reveals His strength through our trials!

NO ONE is beyond forgiveness... Don't allow Satan in deceiving you that you must get right with God first before you should approach Him. All you need is a heart towards REPENTANCE. You will know because the Holy Spirit will convict you.

If you falter on a Saturday, don't allow Satan to steer you away from attending church on aSunday. He will call you a HYPOCRITE and all sorts of unworthy names to keep you away from the church. But that is where you need to be the most. REPENT and God will forgive you and you must forgive yourself. His Love and Grace is limitless, in Jesus' name!

THE SWEAT-LESS ANOINTING! in the name of Jesus.

Lord, answer our prayers today in Jesus' name.

The temptation to judge yourself by what other people say is just another one of the enemy's tactics to prevent you from discovering who you are in Christ.

I AM Praying for You

Meditate on the Word of God and you will know exactly who you are!

I don't walk by Luck but BY FAITH...
NOTHING happens by chance for a believer...I operate by the Hand of God, the Grace of God and the Mercy of God............. ALL PRAISE TO GOD! FORGIVENESS is not a feeling but a DECISION. We are to LOVE our enemies, how? PRAY for them.

Stop worshiping at the shrine of your own success, accomplishments, gifts and talents. The glory belongs to God ALONE. Let them that have ears hear what the Spirit of The Lord is saying... Selah!

There is no portion of the bible that says "And God Failed" ... Because He has and will never fail you can't be put to shame if you trust and lean on Him.

May your days be filled with LAUGHTER and your years be filled with JOY. This is the day the Lord has made and we will rejoice and be glad in it.

"No weapon formed against YOU shall prosper"... The power of BREAKTHROUGH is upon you NOW in the mighty name of Jesus.

I AM Praying for You

Confession of The Day

Confession of the Day - I confess now that I have perfect knowledge of every situation. I do not lack for the wisdom of God for I have the mind of Christ. The wisdom of God is formed within me, so I rejoice! The enemy is defeated! God is exalted and Your Word is Lord of my life!

Confession of the Day - Great is the peace of my children for they are taught of the Lord. (Isaiah 54:13)

Confession of the Day - The Lord will perfect that which concerns me. (Psalm 138:8)

Confession of the Day - Galatians 3:13 is in my mouth. Galatians 3:13 is flowing in my bloodstream. Galatians 3:13 flows to every cell of my body. Galatians 3:13 is forming itself in my body. The Word is becoming flesh, for You sent Your Word and healed me.

Confession of the Day - The peace of God, which passes all understanding, keeps my heart and my mind through Christ Jesus. And things which are good, and pure, and perfect, and lovely, and of good report, I think on these things. (Philippians 4:7-8)

Confession of the Day - I have the Spirit of wisdom and revelation in the knowledge of God. I covenant with You now to always give voice to Your Word. I will never give voice to the words of the enemy, I will give no place to the devil. I give place to the Spirit of God.

Confession of the Day - I have given and it is given to me, good measure, pressed down, shaken together and running over. (Luke 6:38)

Confession of the Day - The law of the spirit of life in Christ Jesus has made me free from the law of sin and death. (Romans 8:2)

Confession of the Day - My mind is renewed by the Word of God; therefore, I forbid thoughts of failure and defeat to inhabit my mind. (Ephesians. 4:23)

Confession of the Day - I am filled with the knowledge of the Lord's will in all wisdom and spiritual understanding. (Colossians 1:9)

Confession of the Day - Jesus bore my sins in His Body on the tree; therefore I am dead to sin and alive unto God and by His stripes I am healed and made whole. (1 Peter 2:24; Romans 6:11; 2 Corinthians 5:21)

Confession of the Day - I, having received abundance of grace and the gift of righteousness, do reign as a king in life by Jesus Christ. (Romans 5:17)

Confession of the Day - The Spirit of truth abides in me and teaches me all things, and He guides me into all truths. Therefore, I confess I have perfect knowledge of every situation and every circumstance in life. For I have the wisdom of God. (John 16:13; James 1:5)

Confession of the Day - Father, I make a demand on my bones to produce perfect marrow. I make a demand on the marrow to produce pure blood that will ward off sickness and disease. My bones refuse any offense of the curse. (Proverbs 16:24)

Confession of the Day - Thank You Father that I have a strong heart. My heart beats with the rhythm of life. My blood flows to every cell of my body restoring life and health abundantly. (Proverbs 12:14; 14:30)

Confession of the Day - God's will is for me to prosper and be in health as my soul prospers. (3 John 2)

Confession of the Day - I am like a tree planted by the rivers of water. I bring forth fruit in my season, my leaf shall not wither, and whatever I do will prosper.

The grace of God even makes my mistakes to prosper. (Psalm 1:3)

Confession of the Day - No evil will befall me neither shall any plague come near my dwelling. For the Lord has given His angels charge over me and they keep me in all my ways, and in my pathway is life and there is no death. (Psalm 91:10-11; Proverbs 12:28)

Confession of the Day - I will not let the Word of God depart from before my eyes for it is life to me, for I have found it and it is health and healing to all my flesh. (Reference: Proverbs 4:21, 22)

Confession of the Day - I am submitted to God and the devil flees from me because I resist him in the name of Jesus. (Reference: James 4:7)

Confession of the Day - I will fear no evil, for You are with me, Lord, Your Word and Your Spirit comfort me. (Reference: Psalm 23:4)

Confession of the Day - I am like a tree planted by rivers of water. I bring forth fruit in my season, my leaf shall not wither, and whatever I do will prosper. The grace of God even makes my mistakes to prosper. (Psalm 1:3)

Confession of the Day - I am delivered from the power and authority of darkness. I cast down reasonings and imaginations that exalt themselves against the knowledge of God, and I bring every thought into captivity to the obedience of God's Word. (2 Corinthians 10:3-5)

Confession of the Day - In Jesus' Name I forbid my body to be deceived by any disease germ or virus. Neither will you work against lift or health in any way. Every cell of my body supports life and health. (Matthew 12:25; 35a)

Confession of the Day - The Lord causes my thoughts to become agreeable to His will, and so my plans are established and succeed. (Proverbs 16:3)

Confession of the Day - There is no lack; for my God supplies all my needs according to His riches in glory by Christ Jesus. (Philippians 4:19)

Confession of the Day - The Word of God is forever settled in heaven. Therefore, I establish His Word upon this earth. (Psalm 119:89)

Confession of the Day - I am strong in the Lord and in the power of His night. I draw my strength from Him, that strength which His boundless might provides. (Ephesians 6:10)

I AM Praying for You

Confession of the Day - No evil will befall me neither shall any plague come near my dwelling. For the Lord has given His angels charge over me and they keep me in all my ways, and in my pathway is life and there is no death (Psalms 91:10-11; Proverbs 12:28).

Confession of the Day - God's angels watch over me. God will satisfy me with long life. I am obedient to God and His Word. God keeps me safe. (Psalm 91:11)

Confession of the Day - Father, because of Your Word I am an overcomer. I overcome the world, the flesh and the devil, by the Blood of the Lamb and the word of my testimony. (1 John 4:4; Revelations 12:11)

I AM Praying for You

Good Morning Holy Spirit

Good morning Holy Spirit!!!
I invite You into my imagination.

Good Morning Holy Spirit!!!
You wipe away all tears;
You mend every broken heart!
You're the answer to it all.

Good Morning Holy Spirit!!!
I rose to tell you thank You;
I woke up to say I love you!

Good Morning Holy Spirit!!!
Thank you for the GIFT of this day!

Good Morning Holy Spirit!!!
You are here!
Let your Grace reach out to me, Here I am!!!!

Thank you Jesus
For another day to Glorify you,
To Magnify your name among men,
To give you Praise!

Good Morning Holy Spirit!!!!
My backup that doesn't back out!

I AM Praying for You

Good Morning Holy Spirit!!!!
Perfect in Power.
Perfect In Mercy and Kindness.

Good Morning Holy Spirit!!!!
My Baptizer, My Refresher!

Good Morning Holy Spirit!!!!
Release Your perfect peace Into my mind.
Fill my heart With Your love.

Good Morning Holy Spirit!!!
Water me, Design me,
Blossom me!

Good morning Holy Spirit!!!
You deserve my worship.
I AM participating!

Good Morning Holy Spirit!!!
You did it again and I AM Grateful.

Good Morning Holy Spirit!!!
My Soul rejoices in the truth,
That I am not worthy but
You continue to love me still.

I AM Praying for You

Good Morning Holy Spirit!!!!
The power that holds the universe,
The reason we live.

Good morning Holy Spirit!!!
I invite You into this Broken Vessel.

Good morning Holy Spirit!!!
NOTHING greater than starting
My day with you.

Good morning Holy Spirit!!!
Breathe in me that my thoughts
May always be Holy!

Good morning Holy Spirit!!!!
Your daily presence is my joy.

Good Morning Holy Spirit.
Let EVERY Living Soul
PRAISE THE LORD!!!!

Good morning Holy Spirit!!!
There is peaceful joy in knowing
That I am covered by Your Grace!

Good morning Holy Spirit!!!
Your love makes me smile.

I AM Praying for You

Good morning Holy Spirit!!!
You are the strongman In this my house;
Glorify Yourself through me.

Good morning Holy Spirit!!!
Because of you, I walk in extreme favor;
Fresh oil and new wine!

Good morning Holy Spirit!!!
Healing is Your nature.

Good morning Holy Spirit!!!
I keep falling in love with You over,
And over, and over again!

Good morning Holy Spirit!!!
So grateful that we're on the Same team,
You are Team Captain!

Good morning Holy Spirit!!!
You remind me of the Joy of my salvation,
When I first came to know You!

Good morning Holy Spirit!!!
Set a fire down in my soul
that I can't contain or control.
I want more of You!

I AM Praying for You

Good morning Holy Spirit!!!
Help me to discern where
You're leading and to only go
In that direction.

Good morning Holy Spirit!!!
I need Your genius to reign in me.
Witty ideas, concepts and insights.

Good morning Holy Spirit!!!
You are my place of quiet retreat,
You are my sanctuary.

Good Morning Holy Spirit!!!!
Give me eyes to see what
You want me to see.

Good Morning Holy Spirit!!!
Thank YOU for the FAVOR
That is ALL over me.

Good Morning Holy Spirit!!!
Thank You for Your finished work.

Good morning Holy Spirit!!!
You are my Oil of Gladness!

Good morning Holy Spirit!!!
It's Your breath in my lungs
So I will pour out my praise!

I AM Praying for You

Good morning Holy Spirit!!!
Teach me to hear;
Teach me to listen.

Good morning Holy Spirit!!!
Your power raised Jesus from
The dead and You dwell inside me!

Good morning Holy Spirit!!!
You are my wonderful Comforter!

Good morning Holy Spirit!!!
Your healing power is great...
Greater than every sickness and disease!

Good morning Holy Spirit!!!
Today, I rest in You.

Good morning Holy Spirit!!!
My confidence is in You!

I AM Praying for You

Praying God's Name

ELOHIM:
I know You can create something out of nothing, please create something out of any nothing areas - the impossible situations in my life.

EL GIBHOR:
I know You are the mighty God, strong in battle. My great defender, I trust You to always come to my defense.

EL ELYON:
I know You are in control, sovereign, and I give You my circumstances today. Take control LORD for my good!

ADONAI:
I know You are my LORD and Master, I choose to follow You instead of the ways of the world.

EL SHADDAI:
I know You are GOD Almighty, and I trust that You are sufficient for my deepest needs today.

JEHOVAH JIREH:
I know You are my provider, and will supply everything I need today and always.

EL ROI:
I know You are the GOD who sees me, and that I am never alone, and nothing in my life goes unnoticed, for You know it all and see it all.

YAHWEH:
I know You are the One and only, self-existent, eternal, covenant-keeping GOD and that You will always love me.

JEHOVAH RAPHA:
I KNOW You are my healer and I come to You now with every area of my life that needs healing today.

JEHOVAH NISSI:
I know You are my banner, please hand me victory in every situation that threatens me today.

JEHOVAH MEKADISHKKEM:
I know You are my sanctifier, making me holy, doing for me what I can never do for myself.

JEHOVAH SHALOM:
I know You are my peace, and bring calm in every storm I face in life.

JEHOVAH SABAOTH:
I know You are the LORD of Hosts, and bring deliverance as You defeat my enemies.

I AM Praying for You

YAHWEH RO'I:
I know You are my shepherd, and intimately care for me even if no one else does.

ABBA Father:
I know You are my Father and that I can run to You and rest in the security of your everlasting arms.

I AM Praying for You

Words of Encouragement

My desire is that you finish reading this book encouraged, strengthened and with Faith in God's saving Grace and Power.

When people say DO YOU, we have only one life to live - NO! We have two: Now and forever (eternity is a very long time). Store your treasure here on earth (temporary) or in heaven. That being said, life is a gift. Always practice spreading God's greatest message of love.

Sometimes just a simple "Yes Lord" can change your life forever!

What is robbing you of your praise? Yesterday's failures? Yesterday's choices? Don't let anything stop your praise!

The assurance we have is that God is Almighty, Able, and Alert! He will preserve you. This God will keep you!

When you're walking in your purpose there is no competition. Your lane is yours, and their lane is theirs.

I AM Praying for You

How I'm getting where I'm going:
Long range vision
Short term goals
A plan for today
And a whole lot of prayer
Help me, Jesus!
Sacrifice always requires abandonment of self.

Despite your setbacks, stress, and disappointment, God still has a plan for you. Your detours may actually become your stepping stones to move forward to your beautiful purpose. Keep the faith!

Best friends are like gold, valuable and rare; fake friends are like rocks; found everywhere!

We serve a God of greater glory. Just when you think He has done something great, you turn around and recognize that He has done something GREATER!

Although things may be hard today, it will get better tomorrow. Have faith that God will bring you through.

No matter what happens in this world, it ends unimaginably well for all who believe upon the Lord Jesus Christ.

Tell someone about Jesus. If you don't know where to start, start by telling them that He loves them.

Psalm 56:3-4- When I am afraid, I put my trust in you. In God, whose word I praise, in God I trust; I shall not be afraid. What can flesh do to me?

When God speaks, who can argue with him? Who can challenge the authority of God in your life? (Job 38-41)

The God that shuts the mouth of lions (Daniel 6:22) will shut the mouth of all those trying to kill God's purpose and destiny for your life.

Every mountain and every hill shall bow to the word of God and every valley shall be lifted up concerning your life (Isaiah 40:4) as Joseph's family bowed to him (Genesis 42:5-7) being the prince of Egypt as you are the royal priesthood of God, a holy nation and a peculiar people as within you line generations to birth. (1 Peter 2:9)

You shall overcome every obstacle and scale every blockage and wall of limitations for within you lie greatness for you are born of God. (1 John 5:4)

All creation will bow before God to answer you and obey your bidding to the Glory of God in your life. (Philippians 2:10)

Stand and speak with boldness in Christ Jesus and do not fear the faces of the naysayers or nor that of the enemies of progress. (Acts 5:20)

The heavens and the earth are waiting for your shining. Shine with grace, splendor, and power. (Isaiah 60)

For this is who you are, a champion of nations, a glory carrier, a fire kindler, mountain lifter, and obstacle crusher! (Genesis 12:2)

Always pray to have eyes that see the best in people, a heart that forgives the worst, a mind that forgets the bad, and a soul that never loses faith in God.

Want to see if something's an idol in your life? Check how you respond when that thing stops serving it's purpose.

New day. New blessings. Thank you JESUS!

The longer you walk with Christ, the more you'll see how narrow the road really is... It's like a funnel. The more we seek God, the more he narrows the funnel, scraping more and more of this world off of us as we go. I am rubbed raw for I want to cling to some of the comforts. Yet I know that by releasing them to God, I am divesting myself of one less thing that distracts me from worshiping and trusting my Lord. If God allows me to find comfort in something I've let go, it's a gift of His love.

God isn't looking for us to be perfect all the time, but He is looking for us to call on Him. Let Him be your strength and help in all things.

Live every day conscious of God's glorious presence around you. He's the same God who built a wall of fire and a hedge of protection around you. He's on your side. You know this because in His presence, there is a fullness of joy, at His right hand, there are pleasures forevermore.

The truth is that you are not a loser. You are not a failure. You are not the scum of the earth. You are not worthless, senseless, neither are you a coward or boneless. You are not a misfit, a reject, a pest or a monster. You are not poor, backward, old, outdated, Oh you are not secluded, abandoned, choked, suppressed, oppressed or depressed. Let the truth be told, yes, you are not an idiot, a fool, crazy, dried up or hopeless. You are powerful, full of wisdom and manifesting the glory of God. Yes, the grace of God is over you to prosper, ignite with fire and glow and radiate in success and flourish in plenty.

Indeed, you are the best of the bests, God's royalty, the mysterious wonder of God. You possess the power to distill the yoke breaking anointing of God. You are more than a conqueror. You are called faithful, righteous and holy.

You are free and not bound, you have excess and more than enough. You are the apples of the eyes of God. Untouchable and indestructible.

You are victorious, elevated, promoted and decorated with divine grace and unlimited virtues for upward lifting and destiny securing. You are a proof producer. You have been rescued from death, shame and defeat.

Know that God knows you as He has imprinted your name in the palm of His hands. Yes, He loves you, for he died for you. He seeks you and desires an intimate relationship with you. He has called you from the kingdom of darkness into His marvelous light. Go forth and shine. It is your time of blessing and refreshing!

"Believe in the LORD your God, and you will be able to stand firm. Believe in his prophets, and you will succeed." (2 Chronicles 20:20)

No matter what uncertainty is happening around you, be certain of this, God is faithful, and He has plans for your good: plans to give you hope and a future.

The Word of God tells us that without vision, people perish. Let God's Word shape your vision for the future and trust that He is at work.

The God I serve is available 24/7
No appointment necessary and He doesn't cost a thing... All sufficient God!

God has never lost control. Our trust, and our hope is in serving a never changing God!

You've been chosen as the object of God's love. He wants to lavish His love on you & love always gives. He has given you His faith so you can believe His Word. So don't try to live your life. Let Him live His

life through you and your faith will always get whatever you need.

God is bigger and better than first place in your life - He is your Life!

When a door in your life closes, be thankful. It may seem like a disappointment, but consider it a reappointment.

For the LORD your God *is* He who goes with you, to fight for you against your enemies, to save you (Deuteronomy 20:4). We always have a reason to praise Him, whether in the valley or on the mountaintop. He is always leading us to a place of victory.

Do what you can do, and God will do what you can't. Do your best in the natural and watch God show up in the supernatural!

Sometimes there is a hidden beauty in the way we fall, a hidden blessing every time we fail because sometimes God destroys our plans before our plans destroy us.

Speaking faith isn't about getting what you want; it's about getting in agreement with what God wants for you! Let God direct your prayers according to His perfect will.

Celebrate the blessings of others. Trust that if God did it for someone else, He'll do it for you.

Count your blessings and name each and every one of them one after the other, only then will you realize that God has actually been faithful to His word.

If you are feeling dissatisfied with where you are in life, that's a sign that God is calling you to a higher place.

Let the words of my mouth and the meditation of my heart Be acceptable in Your sight, O LORD, my strength and my Redeemer (Psalm 19:14). Out of the heart, the mouth speaks. That means, whatever truth we hold in our hearts will show up in our words. Take inventory of what you are saying and ask the Father to search your heart.

There's a level of authority that causes devils to submit themselves without you saying anything, there's a level of the anointing that causes things to shift in the atmosphere as soon as you show up.

And my God shall supply all your need according to His riches in glory by Christ Jesus (Philippians 4:19). We serve an unlimited God with unlimited resources and unlimited ability. When we are in alignment with Him, our lives are unlimited too.

Open your heart and mind to all God has for you! But you, when you pray, go into your room, and when you have shut your door, pray to your Father who *is* in the secret *place;* and your Father who sees in secret will reward you openly (Matthew 6:6). When you pray, your words aren't just going into the air, your prayers are going to the ears of almighty God. He hears, and He will answer!

Today, praise Him. It's another day to be led to a place of victory!

For God *is* not unjust to forget your work and labor of love which you have shown toward His name, *in that* you have ministered to the saints, and do minister (Hebrews 6:20). If you are facing difficulty today, find someone else you can encourage and sow a seed in the direction you want to go. Sow encouragement to reap encouragement in your own heart.

God is more powerful than any opposition you face. Trust Him with your dreams, plans, challenges, and cares. He is willing and able to fight for you.

Even in the midst of chaos, the light of God, His knowledge, understanding and wisdom, is able to shine forth and bring a new day, a new dawn and a new season for you. Let there be light!

I AM Praying for You

Casting all your care upon Him, for He cares for you (1 Peter 5:7). When we release our cares to God, He releases His power in us. You are strongest when you are leaning on Him!

People will reject you, fire you, hurt you and even temporarily maim you but when you come through the process of time, you'll learn that it was a good thing that they rejected you for the stone the builders rejected has become the head of the corner. May God's favor work in you.

Delay isn't necessarily God's denial. Sometimes, it's His protection. If things aren't working in your timing, trust His divine timing.

There is so much power when we pray in agreement. Pray with your family today and watch the Lord turn around your story in Jesus' name.

What are you believing God for as a family? Pray in agreement today, there's power in unity.

Things may be changing in the world, but God never changes. He is the same yesterday, today, and forever. Lift your eyes to Him and He will anchor you with His love.

Learn to plow through the dark clouds so that even when you see trouble, you don't walk by sight, but by faith. It may be difficult but you need to break away from the familiar and step into the supernatural. This too shall pass over and destiny awaits you on the other side.

What are you expecting this week? Are you expecting God to move mightily and to show Himself strong on your behalf? Remember: greater is He who is in you than he who is in the world.

When you walk in alignment with God's will, it's a privilege for people to be connected to you and always remember; THOSE WHO LEAVE YOU ARE SELDOM TIED TO YOUR DESTINY.

No matter what you go through or what hell you pass through, hell will not pass through you but instead you'll have joy, you'll have divine direction, you'll know where to put your foot because Christ is a compass for all to whom He has promised a brilliant life, a life abundant.

There is A WAY OF ESCAPE. Jesus is the way of ESCAPE. Find him and you have found joy for you and your family...

No matter what, never allow satan steal your praise. Praise releases the Joy of the Lord, which in turn is your Strength.

We can either focus on our problems or focus on our blessings. The question is, do you want more problems or more blessings?

It's not what happens to you that matters but how you see what happens to you. If you see it negatively, you promote negativity. But if you see it positively, you promote the powerful purpose of God becoming the reality in your future. May you see God's hand at work in your life.

The Lord doesn't look down on you even though He knows everything about you intimately. You can lie to other people about what's going on in your life but you can't never lie to Him. He calls you by name and He loves you unconditionally.

Peace doesn't come from our circumstances; peace comes from our relationship with God. If you need peace today, call on Him and He will lift you up.

So the last will be first, and the first last (Matthew 20:16). Just because you aren't first right now doesn't mean you can't get ahead. God will complete the good work He began in you.

God sees your tears at night. He sees your pain in the morning. He understands your plight and your problem. He understands how you feel and that you sometimes doubt that He is even there or that He even cares. Know this for a fact - He sees you and He's there with you.

We don't compete in God's kingdom. We complement one another and join forces to glorify Jesus. Iron sharpens Iron in our kingdom!

Today, let your prayer be, "God, use me to be a blessing to someone. Help me share light and love everywhere I go."

Reach out to the poor. Preach the gospel of the kingdom. Pray for the sick, and win souls for the kingdom. This is our season to ARISE and SHINE!

God gives you vision to hold you together and to help you see what's in front even if your circumstances suggest that you're going to be crippled or crushed. In the midst of trouble, because you have light; you won't believe your 5 senses, you'll believe your vision.

I AM Praying for You

No matter how things look around you, what matters most is what's happening in you. Don't let fear take hold in your mind. Cast out doubt by trusting God.

Jesus sees exactly where you are. He sees your dilemma & your difficulties. He also sees the end from the beginning, so that He knows that whilst you may be in some trouble now, it is only for a little while. He is working it all out for your good and you will emerge victorious.

God recognizes when you notice the needs of others. When compassion moves you to help others, that's God moving through you.

Enjoy your trouble. Enjoy it, don't endure it. Enjoy it because it's taking you somewhere. In hindsight, you are going to look back at the last 5, 10 years of your life and you'll say it was good, that trouble was good for me. I declare that it's all about to turn in your favor. God gets the glory!

Every hardship is an opportunity for a TESTIMONY...

Our Praise can alter the ATMOSPHERE !
"David built an altar there to the Lord and sacrificed burnt offerings and peace offerings. And the Lord answered his prayer for the land, and the plague on Israel was stopped." (2 Samuel 24:25)

They may mean it for evil, but like the case of Joseph, God will use it for your good.

In the presence of the Lord is everything you need. He is your strength, your help, your healer, your deliverer, your provider.

If they're picking on you, they're picking on the wrong person because whether they realize it or not, you're not your own. You're always armed and dangerous. God is your weapon of war. He's your very present help.

Things may not seem good today, but God is good, and He is working all things together for your good. He's done it before and He'll do it again!

Let no one despise your youth, but be an example to the believers in word, in conduct, in love, in spirit,fn in faith, in purity (1 Timothy 4:12). Today, remember that you are an example of faith to someone. The way you live your life matters, and you are influencing others even when you can't see it.

You can sense that you're about to step into something but you can't see how. You know that God's about to do something in your life but you don't know which way to go or to turn. Believe it even though you cannot see it with your eyes. Be expectant, something is about to happen.

Make a joyful shout to the LORD, all you lands! Serve the LORD with gladness; Come before His presence with singing (Psalm 100:1-2). The presence of God is powerful! It gives us peace, joy, strength, and so much more. Enter His presence today with thanksgiving and praise!

Perfect love casts out all fear. Receive God's perfect love for you and let Him drive out all fear.

Your faith fuels your future. Choose your spouse carefully! Choose your close friends intentionally!

Those who have access to you matter, and in order to fulfil your destiny, you must surround yourself with people who will feed your faith and not your doubt.

For I, the LORD, love justice; I hate robbery for burnt offering; I will direct their work in truth, And will make with them an everlasting covenant (Isaiah 61:8). Even though life is not always fair, God is always fair. He is a God of justice, and He is the one who is working with you in the midst of your difficulties.

God can do a lot with the little you have in your hand. Faith, the size of a mustard seed, can move mountains. When you dedicate your resources to Him, He will bless and multiply them.

I AM Praying for You

Don't live in regret. Don't let lost opportunities make you feel disappointed and discouraged. God is bigger than your lost opportunities. He can still get you where you need to go in life.

Make time to have continuing conversations with God through prayer and His word every day. The Righteous live by faith, not by cheap talk; faith comes by continuously listening to God as He speaks. Listen to Him; obey His every word and your destiny won't be destroyed but fulfilled.

Fight for joy in God. Having joy in God means finding your rest in Him no matter what is happening. Whilst the world is trying to get you to rest in your career, a business, wealth or even your spouse, you must find your rest in God knowing that He is your joy and peace.

You've been tremendously graced by God but sometimes you wonder why it doesn't seem to manifest in your life. Grace will not manifest without faith. There is nothing you need to prosper that's not already yours. Today, I pray you take all that's yours through grace by faith.

Sometimes Friends, what God sees is the character and not the imperfection of a person. He looks beyond the stammer or stutter (Moses) to the heart.

I AM Praying for You

When you see God choosing imperfect people to do impossible tasks, there is likely something more to them than meets the eye - Character!

Today might not be your day but your day will surely come. Don't take what men consider to be the losses of today to be a real loss; it was a lesson and not a loss. Take some value from it, learn from it and get yourself ready. In God's time, it will happen.

Make time to have continuing conversations with God through prayer and His Word every day. The Righteous live by faith, not by cheap talk; faith comes by continuously listening to God as He speaks. Listen to Him; obey His every word and your destiny won't be destroyed but fulfilled.

Prepare for what you have been praying for. The blessings are about to overtake you one by one. I believe this is your season of increase.

Fight for joy in God. Having joy in God means finding your rest in Him no matter what is happening. Whilst the world is trying to get you to rest in your career, a business, wealth or even your spouse, you must find your rest in God knowing that He is your joy and peace.

God knows everything you will ever go through.

I AM Praying for You

Nothing takes God by surprise so rest assured, HE has a plan for you. A plan to prosper and not to harm you! Today seek the Lord's face and find out His plan for you!

No matter what you have heard or experienced, here is the truth: You are who God says you are, you can do what God says you can do and you can have what God says you can have!

You've been tremendously graced by God but sometimes you wonder why it doesn't seem to manifest in your life. Grace will not manifest without faith. There is nothing you need to prosper that's not already yours. Today, I pray you take all that's yours through grace by faith.

God has something amazing in front of you; amazing people, opportunities, influence, resources. He has something that you have never seen, something more rewarding and more fulfilling than you have ever dreamed. All you have to do is keep moving forward and do not give up.

You are going to need to remember this: Obstacles may be able to slow you down, but they do not have the POWER to stop YOU!
You are an OVERCOMER!
Sometimes Friends, what God sees is the character

and not the imperfection of a person. He looks beyond the stammer or stutter (Moses) to the heart. When you see God choosing imperfect people to do impossible tasks, there is likely something more to them than meets the eye - Character!

Ask God for discernment in all of your relationships today and live out your dream with the people God has strategically put in your life.

You are more than capable of getting it done! Today believe in the fact that God has given you all the resources to accomplish your goals and to win! You are more than CAPABLE!

Today might not be your day but your day will surely come. Don't take what men consider to be the losses of today to be a real loss; it was a lesson and not a loss. Take some value from it, learn from it and get yourself ready. In God's time, it will happen.

There's power in the Name of Jesus to:
-Save
-Heal
-Deliver
-Provide
-Mend broken hearts Name it…
There's power in the Name of Jesus!!!

The Lord is your present help in the time of trouble.

I AM Praying for You

Whatever you are facing the Lord will guide you and lead you through it. You will come out stronger.. smarter.. and Victorious!

Is your name written in the Lamb's Book of Life? Today is a good day to say yes to Jesus!

-Janet Oyebode

I AM Praying for You

Testimonial

Whenever we reach for a book, we are usually in search of something- be it knowledge, comfort, guidance or just simply, a distraction from life's daily struggle. This book with its mix of prayers, scripture and words of encouragement will bring you comfort, solace and a calmness of spirit as you juggle through everyday life. Grab a copy for yourself, your family and your friends!

Prisca Onwenu, RN, BSN

I AM Praying for You

www.ingramcontent.com/pod-product-compliance
Lightning Source LLC
Chambersburg PA
CBHW031213090426
42736CB00009B/898